Airplanes

Gail Saunders-Smith
AR B.L.: 1.5
Points: 0.5   LG

Airplanes

by
Gail Saunders-Smith

Pebble Books
an imprint of Capstone Press

Pebble Books are published by Capstone Press
151 Good Counsel Drive, P.O. Box 669, Mankato, Minnesota 56002
www.capstonepress.com

2 3 4 5 6 07 06 05 04 03 02

Library of Congress Cataloging-in-Publication Data
Saunders-Smith, Gail.
    Airplanes / by Gail Saunders-Smith.
    p. cm.—(Transportation)
    Includes bibliographical references and index.
    Summary: In simple text and photographs, describes several different kinds of
airplanes, including paper airplanes, biplanes, and jets.
    ISBN-13: 978-1-56065-498-8 (hardcover)
    ISBN-10: 1-56065-498-8 (hardcover)
    ISBN-13: 978-1-56065-969-3 (softcover pbk.)
    ISBN-10: 1-56065-969-6 (softcover pbk.)
    1. Airplanes—Juvenile literature. [1. Airplanes.] I. Title.
TL547.S332 1997
629.13—dc21

97-23584
CIP
AC

Editorial Credits

Lois Wallentine, editor; Timothy Halldin and James Franklin,
design; Michelle L. Norstad, photo research

Photo Credits

Michael Green, 20
Mike Stokka, 4
Unicorn Stock/Dennis Thompson, cover, 1, 6, 8; Rod Furgason, 10
Valan Photos/Francis Lepine, 12; J.A. Wilkinson, 14, 18; Joyce
   Photographics, 16

Table of Contents

A paper plane floats
through the air.

A propeller plane flies through the air.

A biplane flies
through the air.

A crop duster flies through the air.

A seaplane flies through the air.

A water bomber flies through the air.

An airline jet speeds through the air.

18

A fighter jet speeds through the air.

A bomber speeds
through the air.

Words to Know

biplane—an airplane with two sets of wings

bomber—a jet that makes almost no sound; some bombers cannot be seen on radar.

crop duster—an airplane used to spread chemicals over fields

fighter plane—a jet used by the military

jet—an airplane with powerful engines

paper plane—a toy airplane made of folded paper

propeller plane—an airplane with rotating blades that move the airplane through the air

seaplane—an airplane that takes off from and lands on water

water bomber—an airplane that dumps water on fires to help put them out

Read More

Jennings, Terry. *How Things Work: Planes, Gliders, Helicopters and Other Flying Machines.* How Things Work. New York: Kingfisher Books, 1993.

Johnstone, Michael. *Planes. Look Inside Cross-Sections.* New York: Dorling Kindersley, 1994.

Stephen, R. J. *The Picture World of Airliners.* Picture World. New York: Franklin Watts, 1989.

Internet Sites

FactHound offers a safe, fun way to find Internet sites related to this book. All of the sites on FactHound have been researched by our staff.

Here's how:

1. Visit *www.facthound.com*

2. Choose your grade level.

3. Type in this book **ID 1560654988** for age-appropriate sites. You may also browse subjects by clicking on letters, or by clicking on pictures and words.

4. Click on the **Fetch It** button.

FactHound will fetch the best sites for you!

Note to Parents and Teachers

This book describes and illustrates various types of planes and how they move though the air. The noun changes on each page; the nouns are illustrated in the photographs. The verb describes the speed at which each plane moves. Children may need assistance in using the Table of Contents, Words to Know, Read More, Internet Sites, and Index/Word List sections of the book.

Index/Word List

Word Count: 60
Early-Intervention Level: 6